Your Local History

Brian Williams

Raintree

www.raintreepublishers.co.uk

Visit our website to find out
more information about
Raintree books.

To order:

☎ Phone 0845 6044371

🖹 Fax +44 (0) 1865 312263

🖳 Email myorders@raintreepublishers.co.uk

Customers from outside the UK please telephone +44 1865 312262

Raintree is an imprint of Capstone Global Library
Limited, a company incorporated in England and Wales having
its registered office at 7 Pilgrim Street, London, EC4V 6LB
- Registered company number: 6695582

Text © Capstone Global Library Limited 2010
First published in hardback in 2010
First published in paperback in 2011
The moral rights of the proprietor have been asserted.

Edited by Kate de Villiers and Laura Knowles
Designed by Steve Mead and Debbie Oatley
Original illustrations © Capstone Global Library Limited 2010
Picture research by Mica Brancic and Elaine Willis
Production by Alison Parsons
Originated by Chroma Graphics (overseas) Pte. Ltd
Printed and bound in China by Leo Paper Products Ltd

ISBN 978 0 431193 66 3 (hardback)
14 13 12 11 10
10 9 8 7 6 5 4 3 2 1

ISBN 978 0 431193 73 1 (paperback)
15 14 13 12 11 10
10 9 8 7 6 5 4 3 2

British Library Cataloguing in Publication Data
Williams, Brian, 1943-
Your local history. -- (Unlocking history)
907.2-dc22
A full catalogue record for this book is available from the
British Library.

Acknowledgements

We would like to thank the following for permission to
reproduce photographs: Alamy pp. 7 (© Peter Jordan_NE),
8 (© John Hopkins), 12 (© Niall McDiarmid), 13 (© Holmes
Garden Photos/Neil Holmes), 15 (© Illustrated London News
Ltd), 17 (© David Gowans), 18 (© Robert Harding Picture
Library Ltd/J E Stevenson), 21 **bottom** (© Greg Balfour Evans);
Corbis p. 27 (Loop Images/© Steve Bardens); Corbis pp. 23
(© Michael Nicholson), 24–25 (© Michael Freeman); Getty
Images p. 5 (General Photographic Agency/Paul Martin); Mary
Evans Picture Library p. 11; Photolibrary p. 21 **top** (Francis
Frith Collection); Shutterstock p. 14 (© Christopher Futcher).

Cover photograph of Skipton High Street, 1900 reproduced
with permission of © 2009 Photolibrary.com/Francis
Frith Collection.

We would like to thank Bill Marriott for his invaluable help in
the preparation of this book.

Every effort has been made to contact copyright holders of
material reproduced in this book. Any omissions will be
rectified in subsequent printings if notice is given to the
publishers.

All the Internet addresses (URLs) given in this book were valid
at the time of going to press. However, due to the dynamic
nature of the Internet, some addresses may have changed, or
sites may have changed or ceased to exist since publication.
While the author and Publishers regret any inconvenience this
may cause readers, no responsibility for any such changes can
be accepted by either the author or the Publishers.

Contents

Some words are shown in **bold**, like this. You can find out what they mean by looking in the glossary.

Making history

History is the story of the past. Historians describe when events happened in the past, and explain how and why they happened. They use all kinds of **evidence** from books, pictures, letters, official documents (written papers), and people's memories. **Archaeologists** unlock the past by finding old things, such as tools or buildings, that have been buried for hundreds of years.

Britain's time periods

Historians split history into time periods. This table shows a timeline of some periods of Britain's history, with a famous place or building from that period. Many of these are places you can still visit today.

Time	Period	Place or building
About 2,000 BC	Stone and Bronze Age	Stonehenge
500 BC–AD 43	Celtic Britain	Maiden Castle hill-fort
AD 43–500	Roman Britain	Hadrian's Wall
500–1066	Anglo-Saxons/Vikings	Sutton Hoo/Jorvik Centre, York
1066–1485	Middle Ages	Salisbury Cathedral
1371–1603	Stuart Scotland	Stirling Castle
1485–1603	Tudor England	Hampton Court Palace
1837–1901	Victorian Britain	Forth Railway Bridge
1939–45	World War II	Cabinet War Rooms
1945–present	Modern Britain	Channel Tunnel

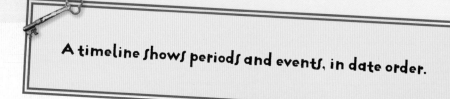

A timeline shows periods and events, in date order.

▲ This photograph from 1893 shows children listening to a street musician in London.

Where you live has probably changed, too. Local history is the history of where you live. It's about your neighbourhood and your family. A person born in 2000 had parents, grandparents, and perhaps great-grandparents born in the 1900s. Their great-great-grandparents were probably born during the Victorian Age in the 1800s. Time stretches back through the **generations**.

BC and AD dates

The letters BC show dates before the Christian religion began. We count BC dates backwards (so 55 BC is the year before 54 BC). The letters AD show a date after the Christian religion began. We count AD dates forwards (so AD 44 is the year after AD 43).

At school, we may learn about the histories of countries such as England or Scotland, of peoples such as the Celts or Afro-Caribbeans, and of empires such as that of the Romans. Each country has its own history, and so does every village and city, even every street. The clues to unlocking the secrets of your local history are everywhere – if you know where to look.

Look around

History is all around, if you look for it. On the way to school you may pass an old factory, a farm, or a house that looks much older than other houses close by. When you set out to explore local history, take a notebook and a camera. Look for things that are old or unusual – a horse trough, a statue, a street name, even a post box. Next time you pass a red post box, look at the initials on the front – ER, GR, or VR. These letters show who was king or queen when the post box was made. They are a guide to how long it has been there.

Ask older people what they remember. Was that old-looking building here when they were children? What was it used for? What used to be where the supermarket is now? Visit the local museum. It should have examples of old things found in your area such as coins, bits of pottery, or old farm tools. It will give you an idea of what to look out for.

Things to watch out for...

- Horse troughs – these held water for thirsty horses
- Blue plaques – these show where a famous person lived or stayed
- Statues – these show famous or important people. Can you find out who the person was?
- War **memorials** – these honour the people who have died during wars
- Windmills – these were used to power machinery to do jobs such as grinding grain

If you come across a grass-covered mound in a field, it could be a barrow. A barrow may be 3,000 years old. Many barrows were graves. Some have odd names, like the Devil's Den in Wiltshire or Hetty Pegler's Tump in Gloucestershire. In 1939, at Sutton Hoo in Suffolk, **archaeologists** dug into a burial mound and found an Anglo-Saxon ship. The ship, and many other treasures, was buried with a dead king about AD 600. You probably won't find another Sutton Hoo ship, but you never know!

▼ School trips are a good way to learn about local history. These children are visiting Easby Abbey in North Yorkshire.

Clues on the post box

The letters VR on a red post box stand for Victoria Regina (Latin for Queen Victoria). GR stands for Georgius Rex This could be either King George V or VI. ER stands for Edwardus Rex (King Edward VII) or Elizabeth Regina, our current queen.

Digging up the past

Exciting finds can be made by accident. You might dig up a Victorian wedding ring in a flower bed. People have found gold coins and rusty swords in fields by using **metal detectors**. Very occasionally, a digger on a building site unearths the stones of a Roman temple. When something this exciting happens, **archaeologists** move in to excavate (uncover) the site.

The archaeologists divide the site into a grid of squares, and search each square very carefully, removing the soil layer by layer. To note where each find is made, the team make maps and take photos and videos. Each bone, scrap of cloth, or broken pot adds more information about the history of the place.

▲ This archaeologist is examining skeletons at the Poulton Project in Cheshire, where students learn about archaeology alongside experts.

Treasure hunting

It's fun to hunt for buried treasure. But you must ask permission to explore privately-owned land. If you are lucky, and find what looks like a gold coin, it may be a "treasure trove" – in which case it belongs to the government. You must check, and tell the local museum about your find.

Scientific tests show how old objects may be. Many old things are so fragile that they crumble to dust when exposed to air. **Conservation** experts protect delicate finds, and most are preserved in museums. Archaeology is skilled work, but you don't need to be an expert to help and share in the excitement. There are local archaeology societies all over Britain that help people get involved.

History is not just about very old things in museums. The first mobile phones look like antiques today. We throw away lots of things that could interest tomorrow's historians. Why not start collecting? Many people's interest in history starts this way. Teapots, toys, comics, stamps, dolls – you can collect anything you like. Your collections could be passed down through the family to future **generations**!

What archaeologists look for

- stone tools – can be as much as 500,000+ years old
- food remains (fish and meat bones, seeds, mussel shells) – can be 5,000+ years old
- pottery – can be up to 5,000 years old
- coins – can be 2,000 years old
- wood – usually rots after 100 years or so, but 3,000 year-old wooden boats have been found
- metal – armour, tools, and weapons sometimes last more than 3,000 years
- cloth – usually only scraps are left
- leather – old shoes, belts, and buckets can be 1,000+ years old
- skeletons – Britain's oldest is 9,000 years old

Some objects, such as cloth or wood, rot quickly if buried in soil. Others, such as stone tools, can survive for thousands of years.

Family trees

Many people's interest in history starts with making a family tree. This is a chart showing their relatives and **ancestors**. It is called a family "tree" because it shows the "branches", or connections that make up a family. Old family charts were often drawn as trees.

Most family trees show people's names, birth dates, and death dates. The example family tree (below) shows only a few branches – four **generations**. Family trees quickly grow lots of branches. Each of us has two parents. This means we have four grandparents, eight great-grandparents, 16 great-great-grandparents, and so on. The further back you search, the more branches your family tree will have. Go back as far as 1800, and you have more than 120 direct ancestors.

A family tree

| great-grandparents | Charles Little b.1930 d.2001 _ Helen Miller b.1928 | Philip Finch b.1921 d.1996 _ Jane Smith b.1926 d.2007 | Paul Green b.1923 _ Katherine Barber b.1927 | Ravi Patel b.1920 d.1969 _ Sally Davies b.1925 d.1978 |

| grandparents | Dave Little b.1954 _ Molly Finch b.1955 | Arthur Green b.1949 _ Sarah Patel b.1950 |

| parents | Amanda Little b.1975 _ Tom Green b.1972 |

b = born
d = died

Kyle Green b.2000   Gemma Green b.2003

Can you work out from the family tree:

1. What were Gemma and Kyle's grandmothers' names?
2. Who were Tom Green's grandfathers?
3. What year was the children's great–grandmother Helen Miller born?

A family tree is a chart. It shows who your relatives and ancestors are.

This seaside family
photograph was
taken around
1900. How many
generations can
you see?

Some people have family roots in one area, going back hundreds
of years. Other people have ancestors who moved around. Some
were **immigrants** who came to Britain from other countries
such as Poland, Russia, the West Indies, or India. Others were
emigrants, who left Britain to settle in other lands such as
Canada or Australia.

Research into family history is called "genealogy". Many people
look at the Internet for help, using websites to swap information,
and to look up **birth** and **death certificates**. It's fun to think
you might find out you have a famous ancestor!

What's in a name?

Names tell us about people and places. Sometimes clues look easy – Cameron is a Scottish name, and Jones is the most common surname in Wales. However, not all Camerons are Scots, and not all Joneses are Welsh. Some places in Britain still have common local names. In Stoke-on-Trent, Huntbach and Salt are local names, but you will also find Ahmeds, Patels, and Smiths. Smith is the most common surname in Britain.

Names of some streets tell us about old trades that went on there, such as Potter's Lane, Baker Street, Market Street, and Fisherman's Row. There are streets named after queens, such as Victoria Drive, and famous battles, such as Waterloo Place. Other place names are reminders of what life was like in the past. Pennywell in Edinburgh got its name because coal miners paid a penny to give their ponies a drink from the well there.

▼ Can you guess why a street was given this name?

The Royal Borough of Kensington and Chelsea OLD CHURCH STREET, S.W.3

"Hello Mr Short, my name's Long"

Some British names had to do with how people looked, such as Short, Long, and Strong, or the jobs they did, such as Smith, Farmer, Butcher, and Shepherd. Some names came from who a person's father was. For example, Johnson means John's son, MacGregor means son of Gregor, and O'Connor means son of Connor.

Many place names are hundreds of years old. Moorthorpe is a Viking name for "small village on the moor", while Beaulieu is Norman-French for "beautiful place". Some names are to do with trees or animals. For example, Esher may have come from "ash tree", and Ely may have come from "eel". Chiswick, in London, and Keswick, in Cumbria, both mean "cheese farm". See if you can find out what the name of your town means, or how your street got its name.

▲ This coat of arms is on a building in York. In the middle it shows three boar's heads.

Coats of arms

A knight in armour wore a coat of arms, like a family badge, so people could see who he was. For example, Sir Roger de Trumpington, who lived in the 1200s, had two trumpets on his coat of arms. This coat of arms could be seen on his shield and armour. A person called a herald kept a list of the different badges. All new arms must still be approved by the College of Arms in England or the Lord Lyon King of Arms in Scotland.

From birth to death

In the past, a name was the only ID (personal identification) most people had. Today, adults may be asked for their passport, driving licence, credit card, or some other official document such as a **birth certificate** to prove who they are.

A birth certificate is an official document made when a baby is born. Everyone born in Britain has a birth certificate. If two people get married or enter a civil partnership, they receive another kind of certificate. When a person dies, a **death certificate** is issued. This system of **registration** of all births, marriages, and deaths began in 1837 in England and in 1855 in Scotland. For earlier records, there are church **parish registers**, some of which go back to the 1500s.

▲ This newborn baby's birth certificate will include when and where she was born, and the names of her parents.

Official documents give us facts about people in the past. Copies of all birth, marriage, and death certificates are kept by the General Register Office. The Registrar keeps copies of each entry on computer files, but also still hand-writes marriage entries in a book.

Ask older relatives what they remember about their grandparents and other family members. Write down names and birth dates, if they know them. Clues to family history may be hidden away at home, in a box full of old diaries, letters, photos, and even school reports. A family Bible, or another book of special importance, may have family names, births, and deaths written inside.

Before the 1800s, many families rarely moved far from their home village. This means that you may find old family graves and **memorials** in the local churchyard or burial ground. You'd be very lucky to discover a Roman soldier's tombstone, yet some have survived for 2,000 years after the Romans came to Britain.

▼ This gravestone is in a churchyard in Over Alderley, Cheshire. It is almost 250 years old.

Gravestones can be useful sources of information. What can you learn about people from the past from inscriptions on gravestones in your local churchyard?

HERE Lyeth the Body of Martha Wife of Isaac Perkin of Over Alderley departed this Life June the 10th 1768 Aged 83 Year

Old buildings

Buildings can help unlock history, too. It helps to know a little about architecture, and how building styles have changed over the years. For instance, a Tudor house (1500s) looks different from a Victorian house (1800s). Local stone or clay was used in different parts of Britain, so that is another difference to look for in an old building. Did the builders use local stone or factory-made bricks? Has the building been altered? Could it once have been a home, a shop, or a farm?

The oldest towns in Britain date from Roman times. New roads and buildings alter the look and size of towns, but in older towns you can still walk ancient streets and lanes that are too narrow for cars and buses. You may find very old buildings such as a stretch of Roman wall or part of a castle built by the Normans. From later periods of history, you might find a Tudor house (1500s), a Georgian-style church (1700s), a Victorian town hall (1800s), an old cinema (1930s), or a block of flats (1960s) – all in the same town.

Watch that date

On some buildings, you may see a date written or carved in Roman numerals. This is how the Romans wrote numbers:

I=1, V=5, X=10, L=50, C=100, D=500, M=1,000

Having a Roman date does not mean a building was built by Romans. People in later times used Latin (the Romans' language) for important writing such as on **memorials** in churches.

If you saw the Roman letters MDXII, could you work out what year the building was built? (Check the answer below to see if you are right.)

Answer: 1512

This watermill on the Isle of Skye, Scotland was built using local stone. Running water from a stream turned the wheel, which drove machinery to grind grain, using heavy grind-stones.

Often people change a building's use. A farm barn becomes an office, a disused church is turned into flats, an old school becomes a mosque, a football ground gives way to a supermarket. Many old castles and big houses are preserved as tourist attractions. They are looked after by the National Trust in England, Cadw in Wales, Historic Scotland, and other organizations as part of our national **heritage**.

Spot the style

Local history is not just about big houses like Buckingham Palace in London or Holyrood in Edinburgh. Small buildings also have stories to tell. Looking at a building's style (how it has been built and decorated) can help to work out roughly how old a building might be. Watch out for copies though. Architects often copy or "mock" an older style, so a "mock-Tudor" house could be only 50 years old, not 500!

Most of Britain's cities have changed a lot since the 1950s. City centres have been redeveloped, with new housing estates, shopping precincts, and tall office blocks. Your local library may have books and photos showing how the town used to look, and older people will remember, too. There was much rebuilding after World War II (1939–1945). For example, Coventry Cathedral (1962) replaced a **medieval** building that was destroyed by bombs in the war. Only the spire (pointed tower) of the old cathedral remains.

▲ Little Moreton Hall in Cheshire is a Tudor house built between the 1480s and 1570s.

Even a modern city may have parts of much older buildings tucked away. Stones from old buildings were often reused by later builders. Some castle walls have Roman stones at the base and medieval ones higher up. Colchester Castle in Essex was built in 1076, on the stone base of a temple that the Romans had built more than 1,000 years before.

Most of the big old houses that survive belonged to rich families, and were strongly built of stone or brick. Poor people's cottages, often made from wood and mud, either fell down after a few years, or were knocked down to make way for better, more comfortable homes.

Ancient or modern?

Looking carefully at the buildings and streets in your town can give you an idea of how old they might be. Here are some clues to help you get started:
- Bricks – used by Romans and from about 1400, but most common after 1900
- Chimneys – house chimneys are rare before Tudor times (1500s)
- Fire grates – iron coal-burning grates were first used in the 1600s
- Garages – no cars in Britain before the 1880s. Early garages were often converted horse stables.
- Gaslight – first used in the early 1800s, some houses still have the old pipes and fittings
- Glass windows – rare before 1600
- Double glazed windows – not before the 1960s
- Thatched roofs – Reed thatch lasts 40–50 years before it needs replacing
- Lamp posts – Victorian iron, or modern concrete or plastic
- Ruined castles – Most castles were built between 1100 and 1600

Pictures from the past

Pictures are a good way to unlock the past. Old paintings, postcards, and photos often show buildings, plants, and animals, as well as people. Before photography was invented in the early 1800s, rich people had paintings of themselves, called portraits. Some people carried a miniature picture in a locket, rather like we carry photos on our mobile phones today.

Paintings give us clues to people's clothes, jewellery, and hairstyles. Remember that a portrait might be flattering to the person in it, who was probably paying the artist. This means that it may not be completely accurate. However, for most of history, paintings are the best picture-**evidence** we have.

A photo "freezes" a moment in time. By 1900, almost every family had at least a few family photos. These photos were of babies, pets, gardens, outings, seaside holidays, and special events such as weddings. Photos, films, home movies, and videos are a record of how life has changed over the past 100 years, and fascinating evidence to unlock history.

Photographers took photos of everyday things that have now vanished such as sheep in a town street, a man making a cart wheel, coal miners with pit ponies, a sailing ship being launched, or a ragged child selling ribbons in the street. A second-hand bookshop or a "junk" shop is a good place to look for books of old photos and old picture postcards.

▲ The High Street in Maidenhead, Berkshire, as it looked in 1911.

▲ This photograph shows the High Street today. How many changes can you spot?

Can the camera lie?

"The camera never lies" is an old saying. However, modern digital cameras can change an image, so we can edit out or change parts of a picture we don't like. How truthful will digital photos be for future historians?

Diaries and letters

When an older person tells you "When I was your age...", you are listening to oral (spoken) history. People's memories bring history to life. Memory is not always reliable. Everybody forgets things, so it is useful when people write about events as they happen. That is why diaries and letters are so useful for unlocking history.

Most diaries and letters are private. They are only of interest and sentimental value to the writer's family. Other diaries are famous, and many people are interested in reading them. Fanny Burney started her diary in 1768, when she was 16. She writes how she saw King George III bathe in the sea at Weymouth, while a band played *God Save the King*! The best-known diary writer is Samuel Pepys (1633–1703). He wrote about his home life, his work for the Navy, the Plague of 1665, and the Great Fire of London in 1666.

The Great Fire begins

In London, on 2 September 1666, Samuel Pepys wrote in his diary: "Some of our maids sitting up late last night to get things ready against [for] our feast today, Jane [the maid] called us about three in the morning to tell us of a great fire they saw in the city. So I rose and slipped on my nightgown and went to her window...I thought it far enough off; and so went to bed again and to sleep."

The next day, he saw "the whole south side of the city burning from Cheapside to the Thames". The Great Fire of London had begun.

Diaries give first-hand accounts of important or everyday events.

This picture shows the Great Fire of London. It was made in 1807, based on a painting made at the time of the fire.

Before text messages and emails, almost everyone wrote letters. Letter writing became cheap and very popular after 1840, when the "penny post" was started. Letters from famous people, such as Admiral Nelson or Winston Churchill, may be worth thousands of pounds today. Family letters, postcards, and even bills, are just as interesting because of the everyday detail they contain. A bill may tell us how much a dress cost in 1950. A letter can reveal what an **evacuee** child thought about being sent to live on a farm during World War II.

Keeping records

The most famous local history book in England is Domesday Book. It was a survey of the land made in 1086 for William the Conqueror, the Norman king, who wanted to see exactly what he owned. The result is a detailed word-picture of life 1,000 years ago, place by place.

An example of a place recorded in Domesday Book is Sandwich, a port-town in Kent. Domesday Book tells us that it paid £40 in taxes and its fishermen provided 40,000 herrings (fish) for the monks of Canterbury. Before 1066 there were 307 "habitable dwellings" (houses fit for people to live in). By 1086 there were 383. The town was required to provide the King with a bodyguard of soldiers for six days. In return, the king had to give the soldiers food and drink – if he didn't, they were free to go home. The town also had to supply 20 ships for 15 days a year.

Old written documents can give us detailed records about the history of our cities, towns, and villages.

In 1086 Sandwich was an important port. In its later history, the town did not always have good luck. It was raided by the French, then its harbour became blocked by sand, stopping trade. It is now best known for golf courses and for the 4th Earl of Sandwich, who is said to have invented the sandwich in 1762 (although he had very little connection with the town, apart from his title).

Most old records, such as court and prison records, and school records, were hand-written. Today, most information is stored digitally, and many old records have been copied onto computer files. Public libraries keep some local records as books, and on **microfilm** and computer **databases**. They also keep copies of old newspapers, so you can read what the local news was 50 or even 100 years ago.

▼ Domesday Book is written in Latin. It names 13,418 places in Britain.

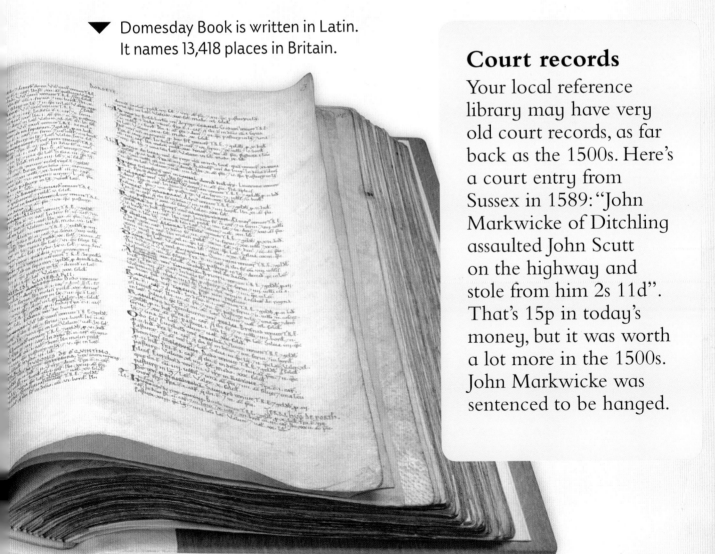

Court records

Your local reference library may have very old court records, as far back as the 1500s. Here's a court entry from Sussex in 1589: "John Markwicke of Ditchling assaulted John Scutt on the highway and stole from him 2s 11d". That's 15p in today's money, but it was worth a lot more in the 1500s. John Markwicke was sentenced to be hanged.

Old and new

Traditions, celebrations, and stories are part of local community history. Lots of places have old stories about heroes such as King Arthur, Robin Hood, and Rob Roy. Traditional songs, called folk songs, are often about local people, places, and events.

Some special local events have to do with religion and belief. These include Christian Easter parades, the Hindu festival of Diwali, Chinese New Year celebrations, and Eid, the Muslim holiday that marks the end of the Ramadan fast. There are celebrations of national days such as St George's Day (England, April 23), St Andrew's Day (Scotland, November 30), St Patrick's Day (Ireland, March 17), and St David's Day (Wales, March 1). Other events have to do with daily life, such as the "mop fairs" where, in the past, servants and farm workers went to find work, or Nottingham's Goose Fair, which is still going after 700 years.

Many people enjoy keeping up local customs. That is why the members of bonfire societies in Lewes, East Sussex parade with burning torches and set off fireworks on 5 November, while on 8 May people in Helston, Cornwall dress up for the day-long Furry or Floral Dance.

Common riding

In Selkirk, and other Borders towns of Scotland, horse riders ride around the town boundaries once a year. In Selkirk, a rider with a standard (flag) leads the way. The "common riding" may date from the 1100s. It also honours the memory of Scottish soldiers killed at the Battle of Flodden in 1513, when the Scottish King James IV marched his army into England but was defeated.

Local Traditions

Here are some more local traditions to research. See what you can find out about them.

- Burning the Clavie (Burghead, Scotland) – the clavie is a barrel of tar
- Oak Apple Day (Boscobel in Shropshire and other places) – remembers a king hiding in an oak tree
- Burns Night – celebrating Scotland's national poet and eating haggis
- Up Hellya (Shetlands) – people dressed as Vikings
- Abbots Bromley Horn Dance (Staffordshire) – dancers wearing deer antlers
- Notting Hill Carnival (London) – Caribbean-style street fun
- Wakes Weeks (Midlands and North) – factory holidays and fairs
- The Cotswold Olympics (Midlands) – "shin kicking" and cheese-rolling

▼ Bonfire societies march through Lewes on 5 November every year.

Local traditions can help to get people interested in history.

Tracing local history

Ask parents, grandparents, and older friends about their memories. What was school like? What was their first job? Do they know any local stories about haunted houses, smugglers, mine accidents, or battles? Ask people if you can look at old photo albums and letters, or comics, magazines, and football programmes.

For tracing family history, the key record is the **census**. A census has been held every 10 years in Britain since 1801. Some census information is free online, but some costs money to look at. To find places mentioned in an old diary or letter, an old map may help. The map will show farms and fields where there are now housing estates, and country lanes that are now busy roads.

Local museums and libraries will help you get started. You can also use Internet sites for more information about family history, your neighbourhood, or old customs. Good luck, and look after any old things you find – they could be valuable in the future.

Local maps

The Ordnance Survey (OS) is Britain's official map-making organization. It was started in 1791, to make maps for the Army. "Ordnance" is an old word for guns. There are old OS maps and up-to-date ones. They show even small local features such as streams, farms, and tracks.

Timeline

About 2800 BC	Stonehenge is built
AD 43–500	The Romans build Britain's first real towns
500–1066	Anglo-Saxons divide England into shires, which later become counties
800–1000s	Vikings from Scandinavia settle in Britain
1066	Normans from France invade England. William the Conqueror becomes king of England.
1086	Domesday Book, a survey of England for William the Conqueror, is made
1348	plague known as the Black Death kills around 30 per cent of the people in Britain. Some villages never recover.
1666	The Great Fire of London
1791	The Ordnance Survey is set up to make maps of Britain
1801	First national census in Britain
1830s	First experiments with photography
1837	**Registration** of births and deaths in England and Wales begins
1840	The first penny post. People buy stick-on stamps for their letters.
1855	Registration of births and deaths in Scotland
1914–1918	World War I
1939–1945	World War II
1960s	Start of large-scale **immigration** from India and Pakistan
1964	First Notting Hill Carnival in London
2000	Many towns and villages mark the millennium with new local buildings, gardens, and tree-plantings
2001	Britain's most recent census. The next one will be in 2011.

Glossary

ancestor person of an earlier generation to whom you are related

archaeologist expert in archaeology, the study of the past from evidence often found beneath the soil or under the sea

birth certificate official document with name, date, and place of birth

census official count of a country's population

conservation preserving an object by keeping it in conditions suited to it

database set of information, usually held on computer

death certificate official document with the name, date, and cause of death of a person

emigrant person who leaves one country to settle in another

evacuee person who has been evacuated (moved) from danger to a safer place. In World War II, children were evacuated from towns to the countryside.

evidence facts that prove something happened

generation one stage in a family's line of descent. Your mother is of one generation, you are of another.

heritage history we all share

immigrant person who settles in a country, having come from another

inscription words carved on a gravestone or memorial

medieval to do with or from the period in history called the Middle Ages (around 1100–1500)

memorial statue, stone slab, or metal plate with writing, set up in memory of a person or an event

metal detector device for finding metal objects hidden under the soil

microfilm photos of documents made much smaller so they can be stored in libraries

parish register official record of people living in a parish, a traditional church-linked district

registration recording information, for example births or deaths

Find out more

Books

History from Buildings (series), (Franklin Watts, 2006)

The History Detective Investigates: Local History, Alison Cooper
 (Wayland, 2007)

Websites

A useful website on local history and advice on how to start
your research is:
www.bbc.co.uk/history/trail/local_history/

To search for family records, go to:
www.familyrecords.gov.uk

To take a look at old maps, visit:
www.archivemaps.com

The UK national archives have information on how to start
researching local history in England and Wales. Go to:
www.nationalarchives.gov.uk/localhistory

Visit the National Archives of Scotland's website:
www.nas.gov.uk

To find out more about local archaeology and history societies, visit:
www.britarch.ac.uk

Places to visit

Most cities and towns have at least one local museum. You can find
museums near where you live by going to:
www.museums.co.uk

Index